HAPPY

mother's day

FROM,

____

Mom,
it's your
day!

MEMORIES

for the
best mom
IN THE WORLD

Für die beste
MAMA
der Welt!

Mom
you are my
hero

Mom,
I love
you!

Dia
de la
mamá

BEST
MOM
EVER

You are
ALWAYS
in
my heart

I love
you,
mom

Thank
you
Mom
for
All
your
Love

you've
got this
MAMA

My Mom
is
THE bEST

save this
moment

Happy Mother's Day!
Coloring Card